W9-BWX-598

100 CHRISTMAS WISHES

The New York Public Library

EST. 1911

100
CHRISTMAS WISHES

VINTAGE HOLIDAY CARDS FROM THE NEW YORK PUBLIC LIBRARY

Foreword by Rosanne Cash

St. Martin's Griffin
New York

100 CHRISTMAS WISHES. Copyright © 2018 by The New York Public Library.
Foreword copyright © 2018 by Rosanne Cash. All rights reserved. Printed in China.
For information, address St. Martin's Press, 175 Fifth Avenue, New York, N.Y. 10010.

www.stmartins.com

Cartoon on page 2 © copyright Wade Hancock, "Lions Supporting Christmas Tree," 1949

Designed by Devan Norman

The Library of Congress Cataloging-in-Publication Data is available upon request.

ISBN 978-1-250-29740-2 (paper over board)
ISBN 978-1-250-29741-9 (ebook)

Our books may be purchased in bulk for promotional, educational, or business use.
Please contact your local bookseller or the Macmillan Corporate and Premium Sales Department at
1-800-221-7945, extension 5442, or by email at MacmillanSpecialMarkets@macmillan.com.

First Edition: October 2018

10 9 8 7 6 5 4 3 2 1

CHRISTMAS WISHES

Foreword

These Christmas greetings from the vast collection of holiday cards in the New York Public Library postcard collection capture the abiding, universal impulse to connect with friends and loved ones at Christmas, but the whimsical, artistic, lush, humorous, and sober imagery from these century-old images is a unique window into the past. The cards are from 1887 to 1944, and come from a dozen countries. They represent not just the common instinct for Christmas conviviality, but the golden age of postcards themselves. In some ways they were the social media and email of the early twentieth century: brief messages, dashed off quickly, to acknowledge and maintain connection and affection.

The images on the cards represent the Christmas ideal of our collective imagination, an ideal that transcends time, country, and culture: happy children who long for magic, lighted trees and festive families, snow at dusk, and evergreens, sleigh rides, gifts, and bountiful feasts. These visions still dominate our conception of what Christmas means. We insist on joy, but if there is too much loss accumulated in our lives at the end of the year, we will settle for longing and a poignant remembrance of Christmas past.

We pray, we dance, we sing, we feast, we shine light into the darkest time of the year, we exchange gifts, we preserve the belief in magic for our children, we remember, and we hope for peace. We reveal our humanity and our dreams to each other at Christmas.

We are fortunate that the New York Public Library was prescient enough to begin collecting postcards, which most people thought disposable and unworthy of preservation, in 1915. The first picture postcard had appeared in the United States only twenty-two years previously, at the Chicago Columbian Exhibition of 1893. They were an instant success and demand for picture postcards was insatiable in the early part of the century. The holidays were the perfect opportunity to utilize the new form of greeting, and a quick and inexpensive way to send goodwill to friends and family both far and near.

This collection of early Christmas postcards, housed for over a century in the New York Public Library archives, distills those abiding wishes for the holidays from revelers from long ago and faraway, in a wish for peace, joy, magic, bounty, family, and for light to be shone 'round the world at Christmas, past and future.

As one card in the collection avows:

Once again 'tis Christmas time
Happy bells are pealing,
Bringing tidings old yet new,
Bonds of friendship sealing.

May your own bonds of friendship be renewed this season, and may the happy bells of Christmas ring out from the past and echo into the future, and may these images remind us of our shared humanity at Christmastime and always.

—Rosanne Cash

A Merry Christmas.

Painting Copyright 1912 by Frances Brundage.

3

Veselé Vianoce!

CHRISTMAS GREETINGS.

All Joy to you, the bells' sweet chime
Make light your heart at Christmas-time.

5

It's more than "Merry Christmas"
that I am wishing you,
It's "Bright and Happy Every Day"
the coming twelve months through.

Greetings to our friends at Christmas, and kind wishes for all the joys the season brings

N.Y. PUBLIC LIBRARY
PICTURE COLLECTION

A merry CHRISTMAS

My dear little Friend :—

Just a line from Santa to tell you
I am looking up all the little boys and
girls I will call upon, so if you want
me to stop at your house you must
be a real good child.
Santa Claus.

A MERRY CHRISTMAS

Joyeux Noël

N.Y. PUBLIC LIBRARY
PICTURE COLLECTION

A Merry
Christmas
to you

With love and good
wishes for you
this Christmas

With ribbon and holly,
And bravest good cheer,
May you dance and be jolly,
For CHRISTMAS is here.

Fröhliche Weihnachten!

2113

I send the Old, Old, Greeting
tendered Year by Year, . . .
Wishing you a Happy . . .
Christmas & a Bright New-Year

A Joyous Christmastide.

28

A merry Christmas

1903

528

29

All Good Wishes
for Christmas.

A Merry Christmas to you

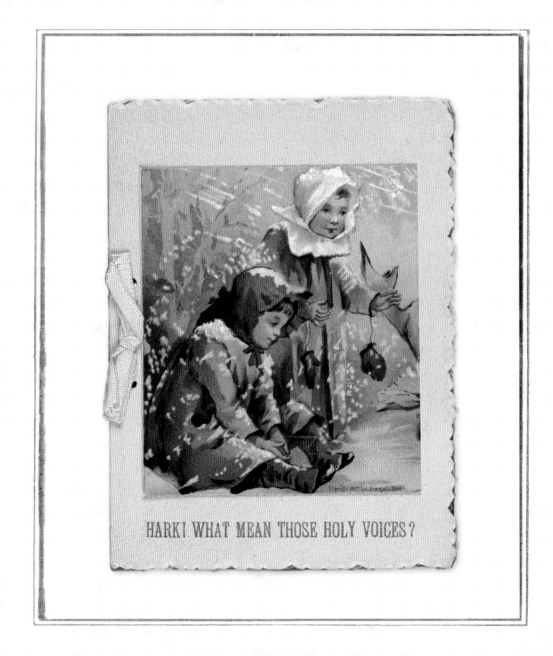

HARK! WHAT MEAN THOSE HOLY VOICES?

A Merry
Christmas

SER. P

VESELÉ
VÁNOCE.

Christmas
Greetings

Christmas Greetings

DESIGN COPYRIGHTED.
JOHN WINSCH. 1911.

Joyeux Noël!

N. Y. PUBLIC LIBRARY
PICTURE COLL'N P. EBNER.

A Merry Christmas

7888

❧ 41 ❧

MERRY CHRISTMAS

I don't forget
        your Christmas
Just because you're small,
            you bet,
And I just hope
        this Christmas Day
Will be the
        nicest yet.

Merry Christmas to you.

We've come with our Muffs,
with our Bonnets and Holly,
To bring you this wish —
"May your Christmas be jolly!"

N.Y. PUBLIC LIBRARY
PICTURE COLLECTION

A Happy Christmas

HIGHLAND COW & CALF

Christmas
Greetings

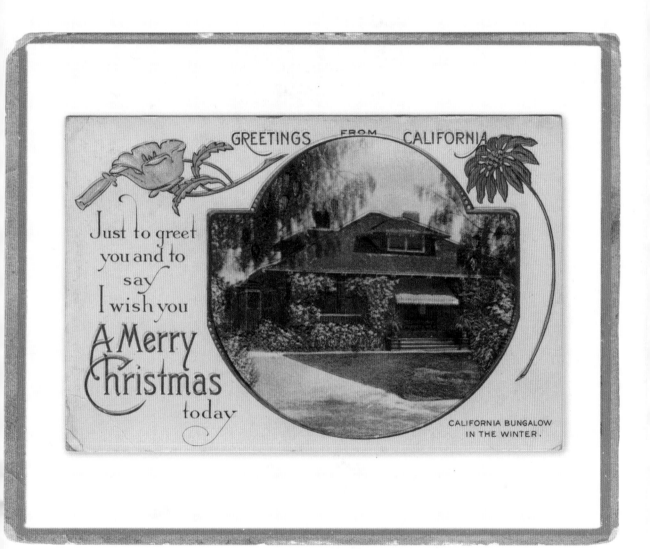

GREETINGS FROM CALIFORNIA

Just to greet
you and to
say
I wish you
A Merry
Christmas
today

CALIFORNIA BUNGALOW
IN THE WINTER.

49

A Merry Christmas.

Painting Copyright 1912 by Frances Brundage.

XMAS EXPECTATIONS.

DEER
SANTY
CLAWS
PLEES BRING
ME A DOLL

Copyright 1906
By The Rotograph Co., N.Y.

B1825

Christmas Greetings

A MERRY XMAS

WHERE IGNORANCE IS BLISS

To The Folks Back Home.

May you enjoy your Christmas Day
In a merry, hearty, homelike way.

A Merry Christmas.

Wishing you a Merry Christmas

A Merry Christmas

A Merry CHRISTMAS.

I've been a very good boy so I know Santa will come

975

A Happy Christmas

N. Y. PUBLIC LIBRARY
PICTURE COLLECTION

A Merry Christmas

"Health and all happiness"

Christmas Greeting and all good wishes.

Christmas
Greetings

To Lucie Freund
From Emily Brown

恭賀新禧

CHRISTMAS GREETINGS

Best CHRISTMAS Wishes.

From No Body.

May all your days be happy days,
But added blessings fall
Upon to-day, that it may be
The brightest
of them all.

Christmas Greetings.

A Happy Christmas

WISHING YOU A
MERRY CHRISTMAS

Wishing you a Merry Christmas

WISHING YOU A MERRY CHRISTMAS

May Christmas with its magic spell,
Make all things happy, all things well.

Christmas Greetings

A Happy Xmas

Fröhliche Weihnachten

A Merry Christmas

May all the hours of
Christmas,
And of the New Year too,
Give health and peace
and comfort
And happiness to you.

445D

A Merry Christmas

We all wish you a Merry Christmas.

CHRISTMAS GREETINGS

AFTER THE STORM

May all Christmas joys abide
In thy heart this Christmastide

CHRISTMAS

Greeting

With all Kind
Thoughts
and Wishes

A Merry Christmas.

WISHING YOU A BRIGHT CHRISTMAS

HAPPY MAY YOUR CHRISTMAS BE.

Dec. 24. 1906.

A Happy Christmas

But I heard him exclaim,
ere he drove out of sight—

"Happy Christmas to all, and to all a good night!"

—Clement Clarke Moore
"A Visit from St. Nicholas"

Notes on Origins

Page 3: Sam Gabriel (publisher), mailed December 24, 1912

Page 4: No date

Page 5: International Art Publishing Co., mailed December 2, 1913, sent to Brooklyn, New York

Page 6: H. Hagemeister Co., mailed 1910

Page 7: Mailed 1908, sent to Gay Head Green, New York

Page 8: George C. Whitney Co., mailed January 3, no year

Page 9: Whitney Valentine Co., mailed 1924

Page 10: Rust Craft Publishers, 1944

Page 11: Mailed 1907

Page 12: Samuel Langdorf & Co., no date

Page 13: Mailed December 23, 1907, sent to Lapeer, Michigan

Page 14: Stecher Lithographic Co., mailed 1920, sent to Vershire, Vermont

Page 15: Mailed December 23, 1908

Page 16: Max Munk (publisher), Pauli Ebner (artist), no date

Page 17: Bamforth and Co., mailed December 21, 1908

Page 18: Gibson Art Company, mailed November 15, 1917

Page 19: P. F. Volland Company, mailed 1915, sent to Niagara Falls, New York

Page 20: Neue Photographische Gesellschaft AG (publisher), no date

Page 21: Raphael Tuck & Sons, no date

Page 22: Mailed to Hartford, Connecticut, no date

Page 23: Wydawnictwo Salonu Malarzy Polskich (publisher), no date

Page 24: A. Noyer (publisher), no date

Page 25: Mailed December 21, 1910

Page 26: No date, sent to Dolgeville, New York

Page 27: V. K. (publisher), no date

Page 28: International Art Publishing Co., mailed 1908

Page 29: Mailed December 24, 1903

Page 30: Paul Finkenrath (publisher), mailed 1910

Page 31: Mailed 1909, sent to Jersey City, New Jersey

Page 32: L. Prang & Co., 1887

Page 33: Erika (publisher), no date

Page 34: Raphael Tuck & Sons, no date, sent to Andover, Massachusetts

Page 35: Mailed 1911, sent to Bay Ridge, Brooklyn, New York

Page 36: 1924

Page 37: Minvera (publisher), F. Molik (artist), no date

Page 38: J. P., mailed 1921, sent to Durham, New York

Page 39: John O. Winsch, mailed 1911, sent to Brooklyn, New York

Page 40: Max Munk (publisher), Pauli Ebner (artist), no date

Page 11: Mailed December 24, 1911

Page 12: Gibson Art Company, mailed December 21, 1921

Page 13: E. P. Dutton/Ernest Nister (publisher), mailed December 22, no year

Page 14: George C. Whitney Co., mailed December 22, 1915

Page 15: Raphael Tuck & Sons (publisher), no date

Page 16: Mailed 1906, sent to Athens, New York

Page 17: Minvera (publisher), Zdenek Guth (artist), no date

Page 18: Wydawnictwo Salonu Malarzy Polskich (publisher), no date

Page 19: M. Kashower Co., mailed 1910

Page 50: Richard Felton Outcault (artist), no date

Page 51: Painting by Frances Brundage, 1912

Page 52: Rotograph Co., 1906

Page 53: Paul Finkenrath, 1907

Page 54: H.W.B. (publisher), mailed December 24, 1913

Page 55: Mailed December 20, no year

Page 56: Owen Card Publishing Co., mailed December 22, 1919

Page 57: Illustrated Postal Card Co., no date

Page 58: E. A. Schwerdtfeger and Co., mailed December 24, 1910, sent to West Point
Pleasant, New Jersey

Page 59: Minvera (publisher), Zdenek Guth (artist), no date

Page 60: Mailed December 30, 1908

Page 61: Mailed 1909

Page 62: Illustrated Postal Card Co., mailed 1907

Page 63: No date

Page 64: F.A. Owen Pub. Co., no date, sent to Vershire, Vermont

Page 65: No date

Page 66: No date

Page 67: Mailed 1910, sent to Chicago, Illinois

Page 68: Stecher Lithographic Co., mailed December 23, 1916

Page 69: E. A. Schwerdtfeger & Co., mailed December 23, 1910, sent to Barre, Vermont

Page 70: Wolf & Co., 1906, sent to East Hampton, Connecticut

Page 71: Mailed December 24, 1912

Page 72: International Art Publishing Co, mailed 1906, sent to Lewes, Delaware

Page 73: 1910–1919 (approximate)

Page 74: International Art Publishing Co., no date

Page 75: No date

Page 76: Mailed December 24, 1907

Page 77: United States Government Printing Office, 1944

Page 78: Mailed December 24, 1908

Page 79: No date

Page 80: Minvera (publisher), no date

Page 81: International Art Publishing Co., Ellen Hattie Clapsaddle (artist), mailed December 24, 1907

Page 82: Mailed December 24, 1916

Page 83: Bamforth & Co, 1910

Page 84: International Art Publishing Co., no date

Page 85: Mailed December 23, 1910

Page 86: Gold Medal Art, mailed December 22, 1912

Page 87: 1907, sent to New York City, New York

Page 88: No date

Page 89: Mailed 1924

Page 90: 1909

Page 91: International Art Publishing Co., mailed December 25, 1911

Page 92: No date

Page 93: Minvera (publisher), Zdenek Guth (artist), no date

Page 94: No date

Page 95: Raphael Tuck & Sons, mailed 1905

Page 96: Raphael Tuck & Sons, mailed 1905, sent to Washington, D.C.

Page 97: Sent to New York City, New York, no date

Page 98: Mailed 1910

Page 99: Raphael Tuck & Sons (publisher), G. E. Shepheard (artist), mailed December 24, 1908

Page 100: No date

Page 101: Raphael Tuck & Sons, mailed December 24, 1906

Page 102: No date, sent to New York City

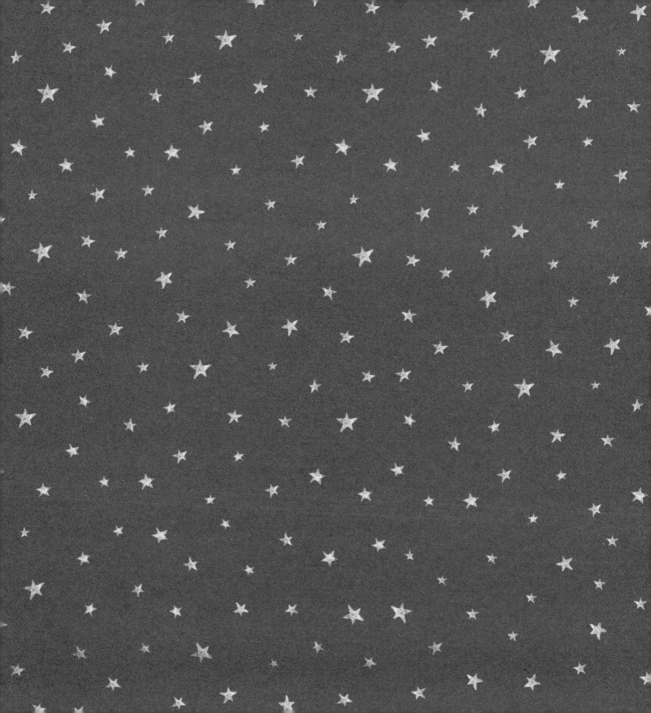